Cottontails

and Their Relatives

Concept and Product Development: Editorial Options, Inc.
Series Designer: Karen Donica
Book Author: Meish Goldish

**For information on other World Book publications, visit our Web site at
http://www.worldbook.com, or call 1-800-WORLDBK (967-5325). For
information on sales to schools and libraries call 1-800-975-3250
(United States); 1-800-837-5365 (Canada).**

World Book, Inc.
233 N. Michigan Avenue
Chicago, IL 60601

The Library of Congress has catalogued a previous edition of this title as follows:

Library of Congress Cataloging-in-Publication Data

Cottontails and their relatives.
        p. cm. -- (World Book's animals of the world)
    ISBN 0-7166-1214-3 -- ISBN 0-7166-1211-9 (set)
    1. Cottontails--Juvenile literature. 2. Lagomorpha--Juvenile literature. [1. Rabbits.
    2. Hares.] I. World Book, Inc. II. Series.

    QL737.L32 C665 2001
    599.32'4--dc21   2001017523

Set2 ISBN 0-7166-1249-6
Cottontails ISBN 0-7166-1252-6

Printed in Malaysia

2 3 4 5 6 7 8 9 05 04 03 02

Picture Acknowledgments: Cover: © Richard Kettlewell, Animals Animals; © John Cancalosi, Bruce Coleman Collection;
© G.C. Kelly, Photo Researchers; © Brock May, Photo Researchers; © St. Meyers/Okapia from Photo Researchers.

© Ron Austin, Photo Researchers 25; © Erwin & Peggy Bauer, Bruce Coleman Inc. 13; © Alan Blank, Bruce Coleman Inc. 15;
© Jane Burton, Bruce Coleman Inc. 33; © John Cancalosi, Bruce Coleman Collection 57; © Lynwood Chace, Photo Researchers 17;
© Jean-Paul Ferrero, Ardea 37; © John Gerlach, Tom Stack & Associates 45; © Patricio R. Gil, Bruce Coleman Inc. 41; © Gilbert S.
Grant, Photo Researchers 5, 31; © John H. Hoffman, Bruce Coleman Inc. 4, 47; © David Hosking, Photo Researchers 43; © G.C. Kelly,
Photo Researchers 9; © Richard Kettlewell, Animals Animals 19; © Thomas Kitchin, Tom Stack & Associates 5, 49, 59; © Steve
Maslowski, Photo Researchers 9; © Brock May, Photo Researchers 51; © Tom McHugh, Photo Researchers 29; © St. Meyers/Okapia
from Photo Researchers 55; © William S. Paton, Bruce Coleman Collection 3, 27, 61; © B. Moose Peterson/WRP from Ardea 9;
© Leonard Lee Rue III, 21, 23, 53; © Len Rue Jr., 7; © Staffan Eidstrand, Bruce Coleman Collection 9; © O.S.F., Animals Animals 35.

Illustrations: WORLD BOOK illustration by Michael DiGiorgio 11; WORLD BOOK illustration by Karen Donica 62.

Cottontails
and Their Relatives

All this growing tires me out!

World Book, Inc.
A Scott Fetzer Company
Chicago

Contents

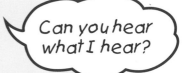

Can you hear what I hear?

Why are my snowshoes always in season?

What makes me stand out in a crowd?

What Are Cottontails and Their Relatives?

The animal you see here is a kind of rabbit. It is a cottontail. Cottontails and their relatives make up a group of animals called lagomorphs *(LAG uh mawrfs).* The word *lagomorph* comes from two Greek words meaning "hare-shaped." As you might guess, hares are lagomorphs. So are little mouselike animals called pikas.

All lagomorphs have sharp front teeth called incisors. Lagomorphs use their incisors to gnaw (*nawh*), or chew. Notice this cottontail's upper lip. Do you see two separate folds of skin on the lip? This is another feature that all lagomorphs share.

Rabbits, hares, and pikas are part of a larger animal group called mammals. Mammals are warm-blooded animals whose babies drink their mother's milk. Mammals also have hair. Lagomorphs have soft fur for hair.

6

Eastern cottontail

Where in the World Do These Animals Live?

Cottontails and their relatives live nearly everywhere in the world. Wild rabbits and hares are found on every continent except Antarctica. About half of all kinds of rabbits and hares live in North America. Pikas live in Europe, Asia, and western North America.

These various animals make their homes in meadows, mountains, deserts, rain forests, swamps, and grasslands—even on the frozen tundra! These animals thrive in all types of climates.

You can often tell where one of these animals lives from its name. The swamp rabbit you see here likes swampy habitats. It is a good swimmer. The desert cottontail, on the other hand, prefers a hot, dry habitat. The Arctic hare lives in the far North. The brush rabbit makes its home in thick, overgrown bushes.

Swamp rabbit

Desert cottontail

Arctic hare

Brush rabbit

What Is Special About a Cottontail's Teeth?

Look at this cottontail's front teeth. Can you think of another animal whose incisors look a lot like these? If you said a rodent, you're right. In fact, scientists once placed rabbits, hares, pikas, and rodents in the same order, or group of animals. But a rodent has only one pair of upper incisors. Rabbits, hares, and pikas have two pairs each. So scientists now place rabbits, hares, and pikas in their own order.

A cottontail's large, sharp teeth help the animal eat its food. The incisors are located at the front of a cottontail's jaw. They do the biting and cutting. The back teeth, or molars, do the grinding and chewing.

Maybe you've seen a cottontail enjoying a meal. You might have noticed that it doesn't chew up and down as you do. Instead, a cottontail chews its food from side to side. The reason is that a cottontail's upper jaw is wider than its lower jaw.

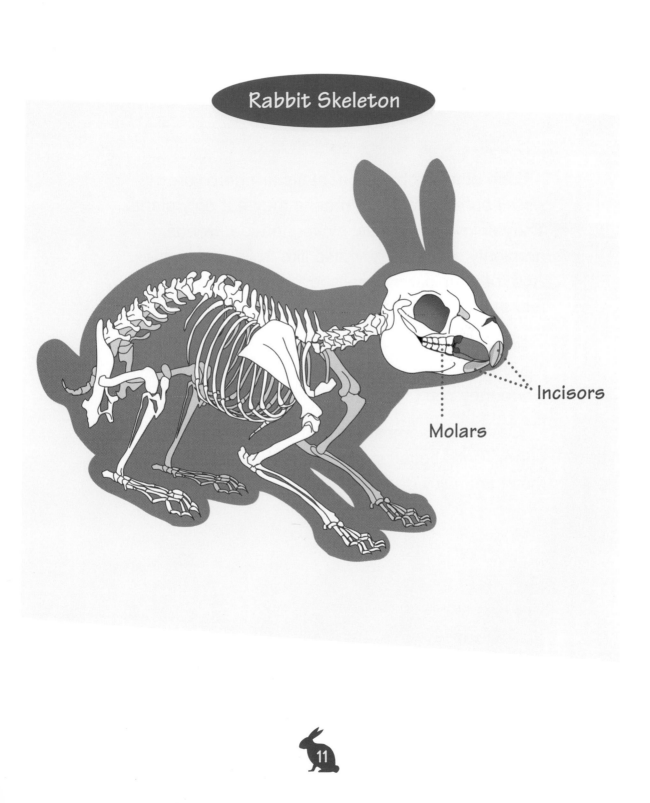

Rabbit Skeleton

Incisors

Molars

What Do Cottontails Like to Eat?

Like other rabbits, cottontails are herbivores *(HUR buh vawrz).* That means they eat only plants. They enjoy short grass, clover, lettuce, weeds, and leafy bushes. They also like fruits and berries. And, of course, cottontails love carrots—if they can find them!

In winter, it is often hard for cottontails to find food. They will eat twigs, bark, roots, and old berries when they can't find leafy greens.

Cottontails sometimes drink water—but not that often. That's because the plants they eat are very moist and juicy.

Mountain cottontail

Is a Cottontail's Tail Really Cotton?

No, its tail is covered with soft, fluffy fur. The tail is about 2 inches (5 centimeters) long. The bottom of the tail is white. It looks a lot like cotton. So that's how the cottontail got its name!

A cottontail is not white all over, however. Most of its body fur is brown or gray. The dark color blends in with the rabbit's surroundings. If it senses danger, a cottontail may lie very still. That way its enemies won't see it.

Cottontails are very clean animals. They keep their fur in good shape by licking it. They also wet their paws and use them like washcloths to wash their fur.

Cottontails take time to clean themselves, but they never need haircuts. Like all lagomorphs, cottontails shed their fur every year. Their summer coats are shorter, softer, and thinner than their winter coats.

Cottontail

What Enemies Do Cottontails Have?

Cottontails have many enemies in the wild. Their enemies include foxes, wolves, weasels, coyotes, rats, and snakes. Foxes may steal baby cottontails from their nests. Weasels may chase cottontails down their burrows, even through narrow tunnels.

Ground enemies are not the only ones cottontails fear. They also have enemies in the air. Eagles, hawks, and owls swoop down on them from the sky. Cottontails are usually helpless against such attacks.

Because they have so many enemies, most cottontails do not survive more than a year in the wild. Pet rabbits, however, may live five years or more.

Cottontail and enemy

How Does a Cottontail Avoid Danger?

A cottontail uses all its senses to avoid danger. Its eyes are on the sides of its head, so it can see to the side, front, and even to the back—all at the same time. It can also see well at night.

A cottontail relies on its nose and ears, too. When it smells or hears danger, the rabbit sits up on its hind legs, straight and still. Its ears point upward and its nose twitches. This position might warn other rabbits in the area to be alert.

If the cottontail decides to hop away, it flashes its white tail at the enemy. This may confuse the predator and help the cottontail escape.

For safety, a cottontail stays near cover, such as a rock or a bush. If an enemy gets too close, a cottontail hops quickly to its hiding place.

Cottontail on alert

How Far Can a Cottontail Leap?

Don't let a cottontail's small size fool you. This rabbit can leap 10 feet (3 meters) in a single bound. Imagine you and a friend were lying head to toe on the ground. A cottontail could leap over the length of both your bodies in one long jump!

A cottontail leaps well because of its powerful hind legs. They put "spring" in the rabbit's jump. The back legs are longer and stronger than the front legs. This helps the animal jump fast, too. A cottontail can leap up to 18 miles (29 kilometers) an hour.

A cottontail's feet also help it leap well. The bottoms of the feet are covered with hairs. They help the rabbit get a good grip on the ground before taking off.

Cottontail leaping

Where Do Cottontails Settle Down?

Most cottontails live alone. They rest and sleep in a shallow, bowl-shaped hole called a form. It is covered with grass, weeds, and shrubs to hide the animals from enemies. Some kinds of cottontails use a form all year around. Others, especially those in colder areas, look for more protected places to rest.

In winter, many cottontails take cover under piles of brush, rocks, or wood. Others spend time in underground holes called burrows.

Most cottontails do not dig their own burrows. Instead, they move into burrows left behind by other animals, such as prairie dogs, skunks, and woodchucks. How convenient is that?

Cottontail in a form

How Fast Do Cottontails Multiply?

You may have heard the phrase "to multiply like rabbits." Cottontails can have lots of babies, or kits. A female cottontail usually has four or five kits at a time. She may give birth four or five times a year. Do the math, and you'll find that a cottontail may have as many as 25 kits a year. That's some multiplying!

A female cottontail carries her kits inside her body for about 28 days before giving birth. The mother prepares a nest that she digs in the ground. She lines the nest with hay and leaves, plus fur that she pulls off her belly.

Cottontail kits are born without fur. At birth, the kits can't see or hear. The mother covers them with grass and fur to keep them warm in the nest. At first, the kits are too young to eat regular food. But kits drink their mother's milk.

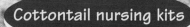
Cottontail nursing kits

How Do Cottontail Kits Grow?

Baby cottontails grow quickly. After about two weeks, they double their weight. They also have their own fur, and they can see and hear. At this time, kits leave their nests and hide in the tall grass nearby. By their third week, they are able to eat regular food.

At about 6 months old, a cottontail has nearly reached its full adult size. By that age, a female cottontail is ready to have her own kits!

Cottontails increase so fast that they can cause serious problems for farmers. In areas where rabbits have no natural enemies, the cottontail population may grow very fast. Cottontails can do great harm to crops and other plant life.

Cottontail kits

27

How Many Kinds of Cottontails Are There?

There are 14 kinds of cottontails. All of them live in North America and South America. The desert cottontail you see here lives west of the Rocky Mountains. So, too, does the mountain cottontail.

The eastern cottontail is common east of the Rocky Mountains, from Canada to Central America. Unlike most cottontails, eastern cottontails live in many habitats. They like fields, forests, and swamps.

The Appalachian *(AP uh LAY chuhn)* cottontail lives in the hills of the southeastern United States. And the forest cottontail makes its home in the forests of Central and South America. Both these kinds of rabbits are much pickier about their homes than eastern cottontails are.

Some rare cottontails live in very special habitats. Several kinds of cottontails are found in Mexico and Central America. They are so rare that they are hardly ever seen.

Desert cottontail

Which Cottontail Is the Biggest?

Cottontails look similar to one another, but they aren't all the same size. The largest is the swamp rabbit, which is found in the southern United States. It grows to about 21 inches (53 centimeters) long. It can weigh up to 6 pounds (2.7 kilograms).

The swamp rabbit shares some of its habitat with a similar cottontail, the marsh rabbit. These cottontails look alike. Sometimes, they even act alike. Both will leap into the water and swim away from enemies. So, how can you tell them apart? It's simple. The swamp rabbit is much bigger!

The swamp rabbit may be the largest cottontail. But it is not the largest lagomorph. The swamp rabbit is about 6 inches (15 centimeters) shorter than the biggest hare. It is also smaller than many rabbits raised as pets.

Swamp rabbit

Are All Rabbits Cottontails?

No, they are not. There are many other kinds of wild rabbits. For example, the European rabbit is not a cottontail.

The European rabbit is sometimes called the Old World rabbit. Long ago, it lived only in southern Europe and northern Africa. From there, European rabbits spread to other parts of Europe. Travelers also took them to Australia, New Zealand, North America, and South America.

Although European rabbits are wild, the ones you may have seen are tame. That's because many pet rabbits are tame European rabbits.

European rabbit

Which Rabbits Live in Warrens?

Cottontails tend to live alone in a form or a burrow. But European rabbits like company. They prefer to live with their family in a warren.

A warren is a series of underground nests, or burrows. They are connected by narrow tunnels that are only about 6 inches (15 centimeters) wide. Some tunnels run as deep as 10 feet (3 meters) below the ground. The female rabbits do most of the digging.

A warren usually has several entrances and exits. Mounds of dirt mark the main openings. Smaller openings, called bolt holes, are big enough for a rabbit to leap into. But they are too small for most enemies to use.

As the rabbit family multiplies, the warren grows bigger. The rabbits add more tunnels and nests. It's like an underground city for rabbits!

Rabbit in warren

35

What Are Domestic Rabbits?

Domestic rabbits are European rabbits that do not live in the wild. Instead, they are raised as tame animals. Many domestic rabbits are kept as pets.

Like dogs and cats, domestic rabbits come in many colors, shapes, and sizes. Each different type of domestic rabbit is called a breed. Many breeds of domestic rabbits are often bigger than wild rabbits. The white Flemish giant is the largest domestic rabbit. It can weigh up to 17 pounds (8 kilograms). Compare that with the wild European rabbit that weighs only 5 pounds (2.3 kilograms). That's a big difference!

Domestic rabbits also multiply faster than wild rabbits. Unlike wild rabbits, domestic rabbits usually live indoors. They don't have to wait for warm weather to raise a new litter of kits.

Domestic rabbit

How Small Is a Pygmy Rabbit?

The pygmy *(PIHG mee)* rabbit is not a cottontail. It's not a European rabbit either. But it is a small kind of rabbit. It grows only about 11 inches (28 centimeters) long. It scampers more than it hops.

Everything about a pygmy rabbit is small. It weighs only about 1 pound (1/2 kilogram). Its ears are small, and its tail is nearly hidden. Even its hind legs are short. That's why this rabbit scampers more than it hops.

The pygmy rabbit can be found in the deserts of the western United States. The pygmy rabbit is the only North American rabbit that digs its own burrows. It makes its home where there is tall sagebrush. The sagebrush serves as food and also protects the rabbit from its enemies. That's a clever little rabbit!

Pygmy rabbit

Which Rabbits Live Near Volcanoes?

Volcano rabbits do, of course! Volcano rabbits live on and near the slopes of two volcanoes in central Mexico. The animals roam the slopes of these two volcanoes, about 2 miles (3.2 kilometers) above sea level.

The volcano rabbit is a true rabbit, although it looks more like a guinea pig than a rabbit. It has much smaller ears than cottontails and European rabbits. The volcano rabbit's tail is not even visible.

To see a volcano rabbit, you would have to climb one of the volcanoes in Mexico. This rabbit lives nowhere else in the world. It comes out at night to eat minty plants, its favorite food. During the morning, you may see it sunbathing in the grass.

Volcano rabbit

Are Hares Much Different from Rabbits?

Hares, like rabbits, are lagomorphs. They look a lot alike and are often mistaken for one another. But the two animals differ in a few important ways.

Rabbits give birth to their young in fur-lined nests, but hares give birth on the ground. Baby rabbits are born furless and with their eyes closed. They stay in the nest for a couple of weeks. But newborn hares have fur and their eyes are open. In less than five minutes, baby hares are able to hop. They are ready to leave home almost immediately!

Hares usually grow bigger than rabbits. They have longer legs, feet, and ears. Hares rarely dig burrows, as some rabbits do. When a rabbit senses danger, it hops for cover. It tries to run and hide from a predator. But a hare will leap long distances across an open field. It attempts to outrun its enemy.

Rabbits are more social than hares. Rabbits like to live in groups. But hares usually live alone.

Cape hare

When Is a Rabbit Not a Rabbit?

When it's a jack rabbit! That's because a jack rabbit is actually a hare. It is one of several lagomorphs whose names are confusing. For example, the snowshoe hare is often mistakenly called the snowshoe rabbit. And the Belgian hare is actually a breed of domestic rabbit.

Despite its confusing name, you can easily tell a jack rabbit from a true rabbit. A jack rabbit is much larger. It can grow nearly 27 inches (69 centimeters) long. That's about 6 inches (15 centimeters) longer than the biggest wild rabbit. A jack rabbit may weigh up to 8 pounds (3.6 kilograms).

Jack rabbits live in the deserts and prairies of western North America. They like to eat plants with thick, juicy leaves and stems. One of their favorite foods is cactus, which holds lots of water.

Black-tailed jack rabbit

Why Are a Jack Rabbit's Ears So Big?

A jack rabbit's most outstanding feature is its long ears. They point straight up in the air. A jack rabbit's ears may be up to 8 inches (20 centimeters) long.

As with all rabbits and hares, a jack rabbit's ears are shaped somewhat like a funnel. They give the hare excellent hearing. A jack rabbit can pick up many sounds that humans cannot hear. It can move its ears together or turn each one in a different direction. You can't say a jack rabbit is hard of "earing"!

A jack rabbit's ears are important in another way, too. They help control the animal's body temperature. In the summer, blood flows through the ears and is cooled off by the air. That keeps the hare cool. In the winter, less blood flows to the ears. That keeps the hare warm.

Antelope jack rabbit

Do Snowshoe Hares Wear Snowshoes?

No, but the inventor of snowshoes probably got the idea from a snowshoe hare like this one! Its two hind feet look like snowshoes. They are very large and furry. They help the hare hop across deep snow without sinking. That's important because the snowshoe hare lives where it snows a lot. It makes its home in the forests and swamps of Canada and the northern United States.

The snowshoe hare is also called the varying hare. Its looks vary, or change, depending on the season. In winter, the hare has a white fur coat. But it sheds that fur and grows a brown coat for the summer. The color change protects the hare from enemies. In winter, the hare blends in with the snow. In summer, it blends in with the soil and grass.

Snowshoe hare

Who Has Fun When It's Freezing?

The Arctic hare loves a good, harsh winter. The animal makes its home in the coldest parts of Canada and Greenland. Winter temperatures there average about -20 °F (-29 °C). Brrr! That's cold!

Arctic hares are well prepared for freezing weather. Their thick fur coat keeps them warm. They have shorter ears than other hares, too. That helps them to save body heat.

Like snowshoe hares, Arctic hares have a layer of stiff fur on the bottoms of their feet. The fur keeps the hare from sinking into the snow as it hops. The feet have sharp claws that dig into hard snow for twigs and willow roots.

Arctic hares tend to rest in the hollow spaces under large rocks. In a snowstorm, these hares dig tunnels in the snow for protection.

Arctic hare

What Does a Hare Do When It's Jinking?

Jinking is a trick that a hare often uses to escape from enemies. It involves hopping in a zigzag pattern to avoid being caught.

Hares can move very fast. A jack rabbit, for example, can leap about 45 miles (72 kilometers) an hour. Some of its enemies can run even faster, however. When a hare is about to be caught, it makes a sharp left or right turn at full speed. The hare's enemy keeps running straight ahead.

Hare jinking

Who Is "Mad As a March Hare"?

Have you ever heard of someone being "mad as a March hare"? It means that the person is acting completely crazy. The expression comes from the way that European brown hares behave in March, or the early spring.

March is the start of the mating season for European brown hares. The male hares begin to leap, twist, tumble, and fight during that time. They are competing for female hares. A female may even fight with a male to see how tough he is. The male that acts the "maddest" wins the mate!

A female European brown hare does a very strange thing. She leaves her babies alone in order to protect them. The female hare can grow to 27 inches (69 centimeters) long. Because of her large size, she can be spotted easily by a fox or other enemy. So, this female hare lets her babies hide in the grass by themselves, while she keeps watch from a distance.

European hares

Which Rabbit Relative Doesn't Leap?

The pika belongs to the same animal group as rabbits and hares. But you wouldn't know it by seeing one. The pika looks more like a mouse or a guinea pig than a rabbit. Its feet are very short. Instead of leaping, the pika gets around by running.

Pikas live high in the mountains of Asia, Europe, and western North America. The American pika is only about 7 inches (18 centimeters) long.

Another name for the American pika is the calling hare or whistling hare. Pikas live in a large group called a colony. One pika will make a loud, whistling call to warn the other pikas of an enemy nearby. Then the whole colony of pikas will scamper into hollows under large rocks to hide.

American pika

57

Why Is a Pika Called a "Haystacker"?

A pika digs a burrow as its home. It then gathers and stacks large piles of hay near the burrow for food. Because of this, the pika is known as a "haystacker."

A pika's hay pile may grow to weigh as much as 18 pounds (8 kilograms). It can get so big that other animals sometimes come and steal the hay. Poor pika!

Building such a big haystack takes a lot of work. But pikas don't mind the hard work. They don't hibernate when the winter weather turns cold. Instead, they gather food in advance for the winter months. Pikas spend most of the day collecting hay, plant stems, and other food to store near home.

Pika with hay

Are These Animals in Danger?

Lagomorphs are always in danger of losing their lives. They have many enemies in nature. Foxes, snakes, hawks, weasels, and owls all hunt rabbits, hares, and pikas.

The greatest enemies for most lagomorphs, however, are people. Every year, hunters kill millions of rabbits for sport, food, or fur. Farmers also kill many rabbits to stop them from destroying crops. And many rabbits die because cars run them over.

The lagomorphs that are in the most danger, however, are the ones that live in very special habitats. For example, the bushman rabbit of South Africa is found in only one desert. Changes to this rabbit's tiny habitat can cause it to become extinct.

But despite all these threats, many lagomorphs are not in danger. Most rabbits, hares, and pikas multiply so fast that they will probably never disappear entirely.

Cottontail kit

Fun Facts

→ Scientists once found a warren that held 407 rabbits and had 2,080 openings!

→ With most mammals, males are bigger than females. But with rabbits and hares, females are bigger than males.

→ Rabbits and hares eat and play mostly at night. They rest and sleep during the day.

→ Brush rabbits will climb into a shrub to escape danger.

→ The Sumatran short-eared rabbit, found only on the island of Sumatra in Indonesia, has striped fur.

→ The bristly rabbit, a rare rabbit of the Himalaya, has stiff bristles for fur.

→ Lop-eared rabbits are domestic rabbits with ears that hang down instead of ones that stand straight up like other rabbits.

Glossary

Arctic An ice-covered region surrounding the North Pole.

blend To mix in well with the surroundings.

bolt hole A small opening to a warren.

burrow A hole dug in the ground by an animal for refuge or shelter.

colony A group of animals of the same kind living together.

form A shallow, bowl-shaped hole covered by grass, weeds, and shrubs made by some lagomorphs.

fur Two layers of hair that cover the skin of certain animals. The bottom layer is softer and thicker than the top layer.

gnaw To bite at and wear away.

habitat The area where an animal lives, such as grasslands or deserts.

herbivore An animal that eats only plants.

hibernate To sleep through the cold months.

hind legs The back legs of an animal.

incisors The sharp front teeth of lagomorphs and other animals, such as rodents.

jink To hop in a zigzag pattern to avoid being caught by a predator.

kit A young, furry animal.

lagomorph An animal with two pairs of upper incisors.

litter Young produced by an animal at one birth.

mammal A warm-blooded animal that feeds its young on the mother's milk.

paw The foot of an animal having claws or nails.

predator An animal that lives by hunting and killing other animals for food.

sagebrush A bushy plant common on dry plains and mountains in North America.

warren A series of underground nests or burrows.

Index

(**Boldface** indicates a photo, map, or illustration.)

For more information about cottontails and their relatives, try these resources:

101 Facts about Rabbits, by Julia Barnes, G. Stevens, 2001.

Rabbit Handbook, by David Taylor, Sterling Publishing, 2000.

Rabbits, by Sharon Sharth, Child's World, 2000.

http://arnica.csustan.edu/esrpp/rbr.htm

http://www.desertusa.com/mag00/apr/papr/rabbit.html

http://www.nhptv.org/natureworks/arctichare.htm

Lagomorph Classification

Scientists classify animals by placing them into groups. The animal kingdom is a group that contains all the world's animals. Phylum, class, order, and family are smaller groups. Each phylum contains many classes. A class contains orders, and a family contains individual species. Each species also has its own scientific name. Here is how the animals in this book fit in to this system.

Animals with backbones and their relatives (Phylum Chordata)

Mammals (Class Mammalia)

Hares, pikas, and rabbits (Order Lagomorpha)

Hares and rabbits (Family Leporidae)

Cottontails

Appalachian cottontail . . . . *Sylvilagus obscurus*
Brush rabbit . . . . *Sylvilagus bachmani*
Desert cottontail . . . . *Sylvilagus audubonii*
Eastern cottontail . . . . *Sylvilagus floridanus*
Forest rabbit . . . . *Sylvilagus brasiliensis*
Marsh rabbit . . . . *Sylvilagus palustris*
Mountain cottontail . . . . *Sylvilagus nuttallii*
Swamp rabbit . . . . *Sylvilagus aquaticus*

Other rabbits

Bristly rabbit . . . . *Caprolagus hispidus*
Bushman rabbit . . . . *Bunolagus monticularis*
European (Old World) rabbit . . . . *Oryctolagus cuniculus*
Pygmy rabbit . . . . *Brachylagus idahoensis*
Sumatran short-eared rabbit . . . . *Nesolagus netscheri*
Volcano rabbit . . . . *Romerolagus diazi*

Hares

Antelope jack rabbit . . . . *Lepus alleni*
Arctic hare . . . . *Lepus arcticus*
Black-tailed jack rabbit . . . . *Lepus californicus*
European brown hare . . . . *Lepus europaeus*
Snowshoe hare . . . . *Lepus americanus*
White-tailed jack rabbit . . . . *Lepus townsendii*

Pikas (Family Ochotonidae)

American pika . . . . *Ochotona princeps*